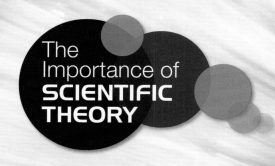

The Importance
of the Laws
of Motion

Toney Allman

ReferencePoint
Press®

San Diego, CA

© 2016 ReferencePoint Press, Inc.
Printed in the United States

For more information, contact:
ReferencePoint Press, Inc.
PO Box 27779
San Diego, CA 92198
www.ReferencePointPress.com

LIBRARY OF CONGRESS CATALOGING-IN-PUBLICATION DATA

Allman, Toney, author.
  The importance of the laws of motion / by Toney Allman.
     pages cm -- (The importance of scientific theory)
  Includes bibliographical references and index.
  Audience: 9-12.
  ISBN-13: 978-1-60152-892-6 (hardback)
  ISBN-10: 1-60152-892-2 (hardback)
  1. Motion--Juvenile literature. I. Title. II. Series: Importance of scientific theory.
  QC133.5.A45 2015
  531'.11--dc23
                                                          2015016549

CONTENTS

FOREWORD

What is the nature of science? The authors of "Understanding the Scientific Enterprise: The Nature of Science in the Next Generation Science Standards," answer that question this way: "Science is a way of explaining the natural world. In common parlance, science is both a set of practices and the historical accumulation of knowledge. An essential part of science education is learning science and engineering practices and developing knowledge of the concepts that are foundational to science disciplines. Further, students should develop an understanding of the enterprise of science as a whole—the wondering, investigating, questioning, data collecting and analyzing."

Examples from history offer a valuable way to explore the nature of science and understand the core ideas and concepts around which all life revolves. When English chemist John Dalton formulated a theory in 1803 that all matter consists of small, indivisible particles called atoms and that atoms of different elements have different properties, he was building on the ideas of earlier scientists as well as relying on his own experimentation, observation, and analysis. His atomic theory, which also proposed that atoms cannot be created or destroyed, was not entirely accurate, yet his ideas are remarkably close to the modern understanding of atoms. Intrigued by his findings, other scientists continued to test and build on Dalton's ideas until eventually—a century later—actual proof of the atom's existence emerged.

The story of these discoveries and what grew from them is presented in *The Importance of Atomic Theory*, one volume in ReferencePoint's series *The Importance of Scientific Theory*. The series strives to help students develop a broader and deeper understanding of the nature of science by examining notable ideas and events in the history of science. Books in the series focus on the development and outcomes of atomic theory, cell theory, germ theory, evolution theory, plate tectonic theory, and more. All books clearly state the core idea and explore changes in thinking over time, methods of experimentation and observation, and societal impacts of these momentous theories and discoveries. Each volume includes a visual chronology; brief descriptions of important people; sidebars that highlight and further explain key events and concepts; "words in context" vocabulary; and, where possible, the words of the scientists themselves.

Through richly detailed examples from history and clear discussion of scientific ideas and methods, *The Importance of Scientific Theory* series furthers an appreciation for the essence of science and the men and women who devote their lives to it. As the authors of "Understanding the Scientific Enterprise: The Nature of Science in the Next Generation Science Standards" write, "With the addition of historical examples, the nature of scientific explanations assumes a human face and is recognized as an everchanging enterprise."

IMPORTANT DATES IN THE HISTORY OF THE LAWS OF MOTION

1543
Nicolaus Copernicus publishes *De Revolutionibus Orbium Coelestium (On the Revolutions of the Heavenly Spheres)*, in which he postulates a sun-centered universe.

1637
René Descartes publishes his mathematical coordinate system and thus invents analytic geometry.

1600
Giordano Bruno is burned at the stake for suggesting that Copernicus was right.

1660
The Royal Society of London is officially established.

| 1550 | 1580 | 1610 | 1640 | 1670 |

1664
Isaac Newton begins what will come to be known as his "miracle years," during which he invents calculus and works out most of his theories about motion and gravity.

1610
Galileo Galilei uses his telescope to view the planets and discovers the moons of Jupiter.

1618
Johannes Kepler completes his three laws of planetary motion, demonstrating the elliptical orbits of the planets, their change in speed and distance as they orbit, and the formula for their orbital periods.

1633
The Catholic Inquisition forces Galileo to recant his beliefs in the Copernican solar system under the threat of torture and execution.

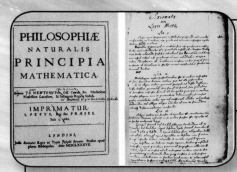

1687
Isaac Newton publishes *Philosophiae Naturalis Principia Mathematica (Mathematical Principles of Natural Philosophy)*, in which he explains the "system of the world."

1738
Voltaire publishes *Elements of the Philosophy of Newton*, popularizing Newtonian theory.

1915
Albert Einstein develops his theory of general relativity, refining Newtonian physics and providing a more complete and accurate picture of the universe.

1700   1750   1800   1850   1900

1776
The American Declaration of Independence, whose chief author is Thomas Jefferson, is adopted.

1727
Isaac Newton dies.

1846
The planet Neptune is discovered using Newton's laws of motion.

1689
John Locke publishes *An Essay Concerning Human Understanding.*

1758
As Edmund Halley predicted with calculations based on Newton's laws, the comet seen in 1682 returns. Later it is named Halley's comet in his honor.

INTRODUCTION

The Origin of the Modern Age

THE CORE IDEA

Isaac Newton's three laws of motion describe the relationship between the forces acting on an object and the motion of that object. By combining the three laws of motion with a description of gravity, Newton was able to explain the motions of the universe, both on Earth and in space. The first law describes inertia and states that objects at rest remain at rest, and objects in motion remain in motion in the same direction and speed unless acted on by a force. The second law is a mathematical or quantitative description of the changes that forces make on an object. The third law states that for every action there is an equal and opposite reaction. Central to the concept of the laws of motion is that all matter everywhere obeys these laws. Newton's laws are so accurate in describing the nature of matter under ordinary circumstances that they are still the basis of physics today.

When Isaac Newton published the three laws of motion in 1687, he began the scientific revolution that led to the modern age. The three laws of motion are the tools with which the motion caused by the force of gravity or any force can be understood. The online encyclopedia *Science of Everyday Things* says:

> In all the universe, there are few ideas more fundamental than those expressed in the three laws of motion. Together these explain why it is relatively difficult to start moving, and then to stop moving; how much force is needed to start or stop in a

given situation; and how one force relates to another. In their beauty and simplicity, these precepts are as compelling as a poem, and like the best of poetry, they identify something that resonates through all of life. The applications of these three laws are literally endless: from the planets moving through the cosmos to the first seconds of a car crash to the action that takes place when a person walks. Indeed, the laws of motion are such a part of daily life that terms such as inertia, force, and reaction extend into the realm of metaphor, describing emotional processes as much as physical ones.[1]

The Science and Mathematics of Nature

In a culture in which little distinction was made between the natural and the supernatural, Newton defined natural phenomena as measurable and predictable. He refined the scientific method into the process that is still used today. The three laws of motion are actually axioms— basic statements that are established as true. But the axioms are only proved to be true when they can be confirmed with experiments and observations. Newton specifically and mathematically defined the terms of his axioms or hypotheses. He used the axioms to interpret observations in the real world, whether those observations were of a falling ball or an arrow shot into the air. And finally he developed a general law that could

be compared to further observations and experiments to determine whether the general theory still held. This method is known as induction-deduction. An inductive statement goes from the specific to the general. It means observing phenomena (falling objects, for example), seeing a pattern (the objects fell the same way), formulating a general statement (all objects fall the same way, even those not yet observed), and then coming up with a theory or explanation (a force causes all objects to fall at the same rate). Deduction is the process of taking a general statement and applying it to specific incidences to see if the

Sir Isaac Newton was an English physicist and mathematician who derived three universal laws of motion that could explain the movement of any body and the forces acting upon it. This twentieth-century image depicts Newton and some of his scientific interests and inventions.

general statement holds true. Newton used first induction and then deduction to determine the truth of the laws of motion.

Scientists today use the same inductive-deductive reasoning. They form hypotheses through inductive reasoning and then use deductive reasoning to apply the hypotheses to specific situations. If all observations and experiments fit the general theory, then the theory is true, even if everything in the universe has not yet been tested; at least it is true until further experiments prove otherwise. In the modern world, all natural sciences—physics, biology, chemistry, and so on—follow the inductive-deductive approach formulated by Newton. They start with specific observations and try to discover the general rules, or laws. Newton's laws of motion basically established the rules for scientific investigation and led to the explosion of scientific discovery that makes modern life possible.

From Motion to Light

In a very real sense, Newton invented science with the laws of motion at the same time that he explained how the universe works. He invented a new branch of mathematics—calculus—in order to describe the orderly laws by which nature functions.

Because of the laws of motion, humankind formulated an accurate picture of the solar system, an understanding of how to simplify the complexity of the forces and phenomena observable in the world, and a way to use knowledge about the world to predict events, alter events, and develop the engineering mechanics that guide almost every technological invention of the past three hundred years. When Newton died in 1727, the poet Alexander Pope wrote, "Nature and Nature's laws lay hid in night; God said, Let Newton be! and all was light."[2] The light was the knowledge and reason imparted by Newton's laws.

CHAPTER ONE

"On the Shoulders of Giants"

In 1543, as the astronomer Nicolaus Copernicus lay on his death-bed, a friend placed the first copy of Copernicus's just-published, groundbreaking book into his hands. That book was *De Revolutionibus Orbium Coelestium* (*On the Revolutions of the Heavenly Spheres*). It represented decades of mathematical and astronomical observations and described a radical theory of the known universe. Copernicus had suffered a cerebral hemorrhage (stroke), and no one knows whether he was even conscious or recognized his book. But legend has it that he was still clutching it when he died. Perhaps fortunately, he was never to know the reaction of the scientific and religious world in the years that followed his death.

Earth Is Not the Center of the Universe

De Revolutionibus, as it is commonly known, contradicted one thousand years of religious dogma. In Copernicus's time, everyone believed that the Earth was the center of the universe. It sat solid and unmoving, and the sun, moon, planets, and stars revolved around the Earth. This was the perfect universe that God had ordained and kept functioning, with Earth the only world in the solar system. Copernicus proposed a heliocentric universe. *Heliocentric* means "sun-centered," from the Greek word *helios* for "sun." Copernicus placed the sun as the center of the solar system. He said that Earth was just another planet orbiting the sun, as were the other five known planets (the only ones that could be observed with the naked eye). The moon orbited the Earth, and the stars (which did not orbit the sun) were fixed; they only seemed to move because Earth is moving. Mistakenly, Copernicus also believed that the orbits in all the solar system were in perfect circles. In his heliocentric system, it was the sun, not Earth, that sat unmoving in or near the center of the universe.

In his book, Copernicus detailed all the mathematical calculations and observations that supported his theory of a sun-centered solar system, and he offered explanations of the way his theory worked in order to persuade any doubters. For instance, he attempted to explain why people have no sensation of the Earth moving. He wrote, "For when a ship is floating calmly along, the sailors see its motion mirrored in everything outside, while on the other hand they suppose that they are stationary, together with everything on board. In

An early eighteenth-century bookplate shows Copernicus's heliocentric model of the solar system. Prior to Copernicus's revelation, a geocentric—or Earth-centered— model held sway in scientific circles, reinforcing the belief that humanity was the focus of the universe.

the same way, the motion of the earth can unquestionably produce the impression that the entire universe is rotating."[3] He also tried to counter any religious objections by asserting that the exact circles of planetary orbits were as much proof of the perfection of God's beautiful creation as an Earth-centered model.

Copernicus argued, "Perhaps there will be babblers who, although completely ignorant of mathematics, nevertheless take it upon themselves to pass judgment on mathematical questions and, badly distorting some passages of Scripture to their purpose, will dare find fault with my undertaking and censure it. I disregard them even to the extent as despising their criticism as unfounded."[4] Yet criticism and controversy there were in abundance. The Catholic Church banned *De Revolutionibus* as heretical and classified it as a forbidden work. Few scientists or philosophers accepted the theory for decades. It was too strange and too difficult to understand. Nevertheless, Copernicus began a scientific revolution in the understanding of the solar system and its observable motions.

Preparing the Way for the Laws of Motion

Copernicus was a genius in astronomy, and many years later, Isaac Newton would credit him and other early scientific geniuses for making possible Newton's discovery of the laws of motion. Newton said, "If I have seen farther than others, it is because I have stood on the shoulders of giants."[5] What Newton meant was that no discovery or invention is accomplished in isolation. Every great genius's work is made possible by the work that came before. And Newton's world-changing insights were based on the knowledge he had gained from other monumental giants of science, whose achievements paved the way for his accomplishments.

WORDS IN CONTEXT

heliocentric
Having the sun as the center.

After Copernicus's death, the general vilification of his heliocentric theory did not prevent other giants from grasping the truth of his calculations and expanding on the knowledge that he had imparted. Slowly, these scientists began to learn about the natural laws that governed the world and the universe, but their investigations could be dangerous in the rigid religious at-

The Geocentric Universe

The Greek philosopher Aristotle, who lived in the fourth century BCE, proposed an Earth-centered (geocentric) universe, which is described as the celestial sphere. Aristotle's celestial sphere consisted of fifty-five concentric, transparent spheres, and each of these perfect spheres had heavenly objects attached to it that rotated at different speeds. Earth sat still in the center of the spheres; the moon was on the innermost sphere; then the planets and the sun were in other spheres; and finally—next to last—came the stars. The largest and outermost sphere Aristotle named the sphere of the Prime Mover. The Prime Mover rotated at a constant speed, causing all the other spheres to move, too.

During Europe's Middle Ages, as its people moved out of the period of forgotten knowledge known as the Dark Ages, philosophers rediscovered Aristotle. Aristotle's Earth-centered universe seemed to fit beautifully with Christian beliefs. Theologians and philosophers saw the Prime Mover as God and the sphere of the Prime Mover as heaven. Earth's place in the center of the spheres fit with the Bible and its assurance that humans were God's most important creation. For the Catholic Church, which was the only Christian religion of the time, Aristotle's universe was the Christian universe. A geocentric universe became a part of church dogma, and to challenge this dogma became not just a scientific issue but also a religious one.

mosphere of their times. The Italian philosopher Giordano Bruno, for example, studied Copernican theory and became convinced of its correctness. He published texts defending Copernicus and even arguing that the universe might be infinite and contain an infinite number of worlds of intelligent beings. In 1592 Bruno was imprisoned in Rome by the Catholic Inquisition and ordered to recant his heretical statements or die. When he refused to renounce his views, Pope Clement VIII recommended that he be put to death. In 1600 Bruno was put on trial, convicted, tortured, and burned to death at the stake for his beliefs. Bruno remained unrepentant, even when he heard his fate. He said to the close-minded, intolerant court, "In pronouncing my sentence, your fear is greater than mine in hearing it."[6]

Church and state fear of and resistance to change and new scientific ideas, however, did not stop progress or the advancement of knowledge. Two of the geniuses after Copernicus whom Newton had in mind when he spoke of the giants who preceded him were the German astronomer and mathematician Johannes Kepler and Kepler's contemporary, the Italian physicist, astronomer, and philosopher Galileo Galilei.

Johannes Kepler

Born in 1571, Kepler grew up a sickly child of a poor family. He survived smallpox at age four and suffered from a crippling of his hands as a result. He also described chronic skin sores and infections on his hands and feet throughout his life. He went to the University of Tübingen on a scholarship, and there he read of Copernicus's heliocentric system with excitement and became a believer. Later, as he was teaching high school astronomy, Kepler began using geometry to try to discern the patterns of the motions of the planets around the sun. He believed that if he could calculate the meaning of the orbital patterns, then he would understand God's perfect plan for the solar system. His mathematical and astronomical skill drew the attention of the greatest astronomer of the time, Tycho Brahe, and in 1600 Kepler accepted Brahe's invitation to move to Prague and become Brahe's assistant. Without benefit of a telescope, Brahe had been plotting positions and movements of the planets. When Brahe died in 1601, Kepler inherited Brahe's position as imperial mathematician, along with Brahe's copious notes and astronomical records. Nobody could understand all the points observed for planetary orbits because they did not fit into the conception of a circle. Kepler followed Copernicus's heliocentric theory and then moved a step beyond.

> **WORDS IN CONTEXT**
>
> *focus*
>
> In astronomy, one of the two fixed interior points that define an ellipse mathematically; the sum of the distances from the two foci to every point on the ellipse is constant.

For twenty years, Kepler pored over Brahe's data and tried to find the mathematics to explain the orbits of the planets. Over the years, although he did not call his discoveries "laws," he was able to develop the three statements describing planetary motions that are now

Tycho Brahe watches as Johannes Kepler uses a model of the celestial sphere to discuss the orbits of celestial bodies. Through observation and calculation, Kepler determined that the planets did not move in circular orbits around the sun and that each planet's speed differs at each point of its orbit.

known as Kepler's laws. He knew, for instance, that it took Mercury three months to orbit the sun, whereas Mars took two years and Jupiter twelve years. But he did not know why. Kepler once wrote, "For us, who by divine kindness were given an accurate observer such as Tycho Brahe, for us it is fitting that we should acknowledge this divine gift and put it to use."[7] Painstakingly and with amazement, Kepler did put that data to use and finally came to the inescapable conclusion that the planets do not orbit in perfect circles. They orbit in an ellipse. At different points in their orbits, the planets are at variable distances from the sun. The theory that planets travel in an ellipse with the sun at one focus point of that ellipse has come to be known as Kepler's first law. It was a radical, shocking idea, even to Kepler, but he proved to himself mathematically that it had to be true.

Kepler's second law is about the speed of any planet orbiting the sun. That speed is variable. Planets travel faster when their elliptical orbits bring them closest to the sun and slower when they are farther away from the sun. Perhaps, he thought, the sun pushed on them in some way, and that effect was weaker as the planets were farther away. Kepler figured out a mathematical way to describe that variability. It says that an imaginary line drawn from a planet to the sun marks out equal areas in equal times, no matter where in its orbit a planet is.

> **WORDS IN CONTEXT**
>
> *elliptical*
> Shaped like an ellipse; oval or like an elongated circle.

The third law, discovered in 1618, is an attempt to describe the pattern or mathematical rule represented by the orbits of all the known planets and how long each takes to orbit the sun—the length of each planet's year. It is a complicated formula that involves cubing the orbital distance from the sun, squaring the planet's year, and then dividing the cubed number by the squared number. Science writer Edward Dolnick explains, "Put another way, the length of a planet's year depends not on its distance from the sun, or on that distance squared, but on something in between—the distance raised to the 3/2 power."[8] Kepler knew it was so, but he had no idea why or if it meant something about God's plan or what his formula implied. It seemed strange and inexplicable. Nevertheless, Kepler's exploration of planetary motion and his three laws represented a giant step forward in describing the motions of the heavens.

Galileo Galilei

At the same time that Kepler was studying planetary motion, Galileo was exploring the heavens with the first telescopes and trying to understand the motions of objects on Earth. Galileo lived in Italy and was unaware of Kepler's work, but he was a firm believer in Copernican theory and a genius physicist, astronomer, and mathematician. Kepler, as a German Protestant, did not face the religious dangers of the Inquisition, although his astronomical works were understood and accepted by very few. Galileo eventually faced fierce opposition to his research, especially in astronomy, from the Catholic Church. Still, he authored the next great advance in understanding motion and the organization of the solar system.

On January 7, 1610, Galileo used a telescope to look at the night sky. The telescope was primitive—just a rolled-up tube made of paper and wood with two lenses such as those ground for eyeglasses inside. It magnified objects only about twenty times, but what Galileo saw astonished him and everyone who heard of his discoveries. Three months later he published his small book *Starry Messenger*, in which he listed his discoveries. He saw that Earth's moon was covered in mountains, valleys, and rough terrain. It was not the perfectly smooth surface that people had thought. Neither was the sun; it was pockmarked with black spots. The Milky Way was not a heavenly fog but

Using a primitive telescope, Galileo was able to discern the moons of Jupiter as well as some features of Earth's moon and the sun. He also could see more clearly that the Milky Way was made up of a multitude of stars not visible to the naked eye.

The Picturesque Tycho Brahe

Born into the nobility in Denmark in 1546, Tycho Brahe studied astronomy in college. He was a rowdy, flamboyant character. At age twenty he fought a duel with another student over who was right about a mathematical formula. Brahe lost his nose in the duel and for the rest of his life wore a fake nose made of brass. Some stories say that he had gold and silver noses to wear for special occasions. Brahe was extremely wealthy, lived in a castle, employed a little person named Jepp as a court jester, and kept a beer-drinking elk as a pet.

In 1575 the king of Denmark, Frederick II, gave Brahe an island and built a huge astronomical observatory for him. There, without a telescope, Brahe made most of his detailed observations of the heavens. He spent years tracking the orbits of the visible heavenly bodies and kept careful records of their positions at given points in time. Although Brahe never gave up the idea of an Earth-centered universe, he did recognize that such a system did not fit his observations. He proposed that the sun and moon circled the Earth, whereas the planets orbited the sun. Nevertheless, his reams of recorded observations, inherited by Johannes Kepler, provided essential data to prove that the Copernican sun-centered system was correct.

a mass of stars. Four moons circled Jupiter. Stars in quantities never imagined leaped into view. Galileo wrote, "After the Moon, I frequently observed other heavenly bodies, both fixed stars and planets, with incredible delight."[9] In his book, Galileo hinted at acceptance of the heliocentric system but did not overtly state it. Still, the discoveries stripped Earth of its specialness. It was not the only world, and even its moon was not unique in the solar system.

Even before 1610, Galileo had been fascinated by motion and had devoted himself to studying motions of objects. In 1604 he began experimenting with the speed of falling bodies, using differently inclined ramps down which he could roll balls of different weights. He also tried dropping objects from different heights and noting when they hit the ground. The ancient Greek philosopher Aristotle had taught that bodies of different weights fall at different speeds, and everyone accepted the truth of that idea. Galileo proved Aristotle wrong. He proved with his experiments that the speed of a falling object over time is independent of its weight. He mathematically demonstrated his law of falling bodies, which uses an equation to state that any object of any weight, mass, or shape accelerates in exactly the same way, and the distance it falls is proportional to time traveled. The math formula says distance is proportional to time squared. Galileo knew that the air could interfere with the fall of a feather, for example, and make its descent slower than the fall of a cannonball, but both a marble and a cannonball—similarly affected by the air—fell at exactly the same rate. He even imagined the idea of a vacuum and insisted that both a feather and a cannonball would fall the same distance in the same amount of time in an airless environment.

Galileo carried his theories of motion further. He proposed that the Earth is in motion, too, and finally asserted for all to read and hear that the heliocentric solar system was a fact. Earth was spinning about the sun. To those critics who argued that a moving world would be chaotic with objects falling sideways and buildings jarred into collapse, he offered the analogy of a ship at sea. Smooth motion, he explained, was indistinguishable from motionlessness. He said:

> Shut yourself up with some friend in the main cabin below decks on some large ship and have with you there some flies, butterflies, and other small flying animals. Have a large bowl of water with some fish in it; hang up a bottle that empties drop by drop into a . . . vessel beneath it. With the ship standing still, observe carefully how the little animals fly with equal speed to all sides of the cabin. The fish swim indifferently in all directions; the drops fall into the vessel beneath. . . . When you have observed all these things carefully (though there is no doubt that when the ship is standing still everything must happen in this way), have the ship proceed with any speed you like, so long as the motion is uniform and not fluctuating this way and that. You will discover not the least change in all the effects named, nor could you tell from any of them whether the ship was moving or standing still.[10]

Galileo had gone too far for the religious leaders of Rome. His science defied accepted doctrine and, according to the church, was heresy. In 1633 Galileo was subjected to a Church trial and ordered to recant his Copernican views and claims about the Earth's motion. Under threat of torture, he agreed never to speak or write such heresy again and was sentenced to live under house arrest until his death in 1642.

Mathematics Will Explain the World

No amount of persecution, however, could prevent the progress of science and mathematics, especially in European areas with less-rigid religious doctrines. In France, for example, philosopher René Descartes came up with a way to mathematically describe changes in motion over time. He said he developed the system while lying in his bed one morning watching a fly climb up the wall. He created the idea of graphs by thinking of time as being on a chart's horizontal axis and specific points along a curve or other geometric shape as on the vertical axis. With x and y axes, geometry could be treated as an equation that could describe observed motion in the world; these are called Cartesian coordinates in honor of Descartes. Graphs were a spectacular tool that moved all scientific studies forward, and they became an essential part of the efforts to define the natural laws that ruled the universe.

Dolnick says of men such as Descartes, Copernicus, Kepler, and Galileo, "All these thinkers had two traits in common. They were geniuses, and they had utter faith that the universe had been designed on impeccable mathematical lines."[11] In the same year that Galileo died, the genius who would synthesize the natural laws that these men struggled to define was born. His name was Isaac Newton, and he would revolutionize humankind's understanding of everything.

CHAPTER TWO

Isaac Newton

Kepler and Galileo demonstrated that mathematics somehow ruled the sky and the Earth, and Descartes developed a system for mathematically describing each moment of a moving object's path and showed that everything could be reduced to mathematical calculations. Isaac Newton not only proved that these discoveries fit together beautifully and simply but also explained why and how. When Newton published his theory of the laws of motion in 1687, he ushered in the seventeenth-century scientific revolution. He established the very essence of science with his exact mathematical explanations of nature and natural law.

A Difficult Beginning

By the old Julian calendar then in use in England, Isaac Newton was born on Christmas Day in 1642. This calendar, however, was about ten days behind the Gregorian calendar used today and handled leap years differently, too. Newton considered his birthday to be December 25, but according to the modern calendar, he was born on January 4, 1643. Born prematurely in Woolsthorpe, Lincolnshire, England, Isaac was a weak baby who was not expected to survive. His father had died three months previously, and Isaac was his only child. Isaac's young mother remarried when her son was three years old. Her new husband, a wealthy clergyman named Barnabas Smith, did not want a stepson, so when his mother moved to her husband's home, she left Isaac behind on the family farm with his grandmother. Eight years later, when Smith died, Isaac's mother returned to the farm with her three new children. Many historians believe that the early abandonment affected Isaac all his life. He was a sensitive, introverted, secretive child, and as he grew up, he was often insecure, depressed, emotionally unstable, and subject to bouts of anger and subsequent guilt. Nine years after his stepfather's death, for instance, Isaac wrote down a list of all his boyhood "sins." One tortured memory of sin was, "threatning my father and mother Smith to burne them and the house over them."[12] He also shamefully recalled punching his half sisters and wishing to die himself (which was a sin, according to his rigid religious upbringing).

Lonely and moody as he was, Isaac was a smart, curious child with varied interests and skills. He taught himself to make sundials that told time by the position of shadows falling on the dials. His sundials were accurate within a quarter hour, and his invention was used by anyone in the neighborhood who wanted to know the time. He was fascinated by geometric shapes and drew circles, arcs, intersecting lines, and triangles in the dirt and with charcoal on the walls. At age ten, Isaac was sent to school in town and boarded with an apothecary (a druggist), where he decorated the walls of his attic room with drawings of birds, animals, ships, and people. In a small notebook, he carefully copied recipes for making salves, potions, and cures learned from the apothecary. He built wooden models of windmills, made paper lanterns and kites, and built a water clock for his attic room. He did well in school, learning Latin, Greek, arithmetic, and some geometry.

Obsessed with Learning

When Newton was sixteen, his mother brought him home to run the farm, but the youth detested farming. He read and daydreamed when he was supposed to be working, and he performed his tasks so badly that something had to change. Finally, in 1661 his mother sent him to college at the University of Cambridge, about 50 miles (80 km) north of London. He studied the usual ancient Greek and Roman subjects, such as Aristotle and other classical philosophers, but the university had also hired its first mathematics professor, Isaac Barrow. And it had a library of some three thousand books. Newton's abiding interests in mathematics, motion (such as the flight of kites and workings of windmills), and time (clocks and sundials) led him into intense, almost obsessive educational explorations. He read Galileo and Descartes. He also read the works of contemporary scientists such as the chemist Robert Boyle, who, with his colleague Robert Hooke, invented the vacuum pump for studying gases and pressure. These men were some of the Western world's first true scientists. In 1660 Boyle and eleven other men formed the Royal Society of London, dedicated to discussing scientific topics, performing experiments, and gaining knowledge through empiric observation.

At nineteen, Newton was too young to have any contact with the Royal Society, but he was living in an intellectual atmosphere that embraced Copernican theory and completely accepted the movement of the Earth and the solar system as fact. Astronomy was a valid topic of investigation, and mathematics was the way to understand the universe. Galileo had said that the universe was the book of God, and "it is written in the language of mathematics."[13] Newton wanted to understand everything about God's creation. He learned Euclidean geometry and taught himself trigonometry. He bought his own books on mathematics and buried himself in them. He found mathematics easy. He remained isolated and friendless, but he was content with absorbing all that books and his teachers had to offer him.

Newton's Miracle Years

Then in 1665 one of the epidemics of bubonic plague that periodically swept Europe came to nearby London. So many people were dying in London each week that the colleges of the University of Cambridge closed, and the students were sent home to escape the plague. Newton returned to Woolsthorpe and remained there for some twenty months, cut off from school but not from intellectual investigation. During this time the twenty-four-year-old feverishly continued his studies and accomplished most of the incredibly creative mathematical and scientific work that became his laws of motion.

Newton had inherited a blank book of bound pages from his stepfather. He named it his "Waste Book" and used it to set up math problems to solve. He invented and solved equations related to motion, infinity, velocity, acceleration, mass, and weight. It was a period in history when exactness did not exist in any discipline. Weights and measurements varied with country and language and were often only estimates. Concepts such as time or force were not scientifically defined. Gravity (the tendency of things to fall) versus levity (the tendency of some things to rise) was an idea without definition or explanation. Even spelling rules were fluid and nonstandardized. Newton had to create his own mathematical notation system and set out to assign mathematical precision where none existed before. He basically invented calculus so that he would have a way to analyze how things change over time. He filled page after page of his Waste Book with equations that led him further and further into understanding mathematical rules that governed nature. Historian James Gleick explains, "He pushed past the frontier of knowledge (though he did not know this). . . . Solitary and almost incommunicado, he became the world's paramount mathematician."[14]

Newton's Waste Book was full of questions. He wondered what kept the moon in orbit around the Earth instead of it flying off in a straight line. He asked why objects on Earth fell downward instead of shooting off into space—or at least sideways—as Earth spun around the sun. He speculated about what kind of force kept heavenly and earthly bodies in their places. He pondered the mathematical rules that might explain movements and forces. He asked himself how to meaningfully define words such as *force*, *body*, *space*, and *time*. And he began to form conclusions, along with mathematical estimates of the force needed to keep the moon in its orbit and objects reliably falling straight down to the ground on Earth. He recorded axioms in his Waste Book, such as:

1. If a quantity once move it will never rest unlesse hindered by some externall cause.

2. A quantity will always move on in the same streight line (not changing the determination nor celerity of its motion) unless some externall cause divert it.

3. There is exactly so much required, so much and noe more force to reduce a body to rest as there was to put it upon motion.[15]

An object at rest remains at rest because the forces acting upon it are balanced. In this example, the ball is at rest because the force of gravity pushing it down is balanced with the force of the hand pushing it up. Remove the force of the hand, and the force that acts upon the ball is gravity. Because of the force of gravity, the ball will remain in motion until it hits the ground.

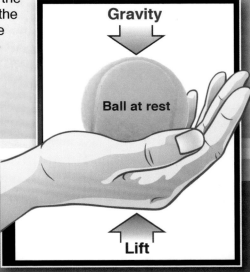

Gravity

Ball at rest

Lift

Source: NASA, "Rockets: An Educator's Guide with Activities in Science, Mathematics, and Technology." http://lroc.sese.asu.edu.

He was thinking about gravity as a force that could be measured and motion as explainable in relation to that force, even though he did not yet quite understand what rules applied to all things. At the same time, Newton was reading a new book by Hooke called *Micrographia*. The book described some of the objects Hooke had seen with a simple microscope, such as plant cells, the legs of a flea, and bird feathers. It also discussed a theory of color, based on Hooke's experiences with lenses and prisms. Microscopically, Hooke had seen rainbows form in tiny drops of water, and he suggested that these colors were born of motion. Newton was fascinated by this theory and also began to experiment with prisms and color. He discovered with his prism experiments that color was determined by how sharply sunlight was bent. Each color separated out from white light by a prism had its own degree of refraction.

The Mathematical Genius

In 1667, with the London plague over, Newton returned to Cambridge and his studies. He told no one about his Woolsthorpe investigations and ideas about motion and gravity. He did, however, share some of his mathematical discoveries with Barrow, his mathematics professor. Barrow was so impressed that he sent some of Newton's equations to friends in the Royal Society of London. Soon some of the mathematicians there were sending problems in analytic geometry to Newton for solution. Barrow praised Newton as a man of "extraordinary genius,"[16] and when Barrow left Cambridge in 1669, Newton took over the professorship in mathematics. While he gave lectures on mathematics and the nature of light to the few students who were interested, Newton continued his own private study of motion and other phenomena in the natural world. His efforts to build a better telescope—with lenses that did not refract as much and did not blur magnified images—gained him an invitation to join the Royal Society. He accepted and in 1672 sent a revolutionary paper to the members detailing his theory of light and explaining that white light was a mixture of all colors, which were separated from rays of light by prisms.

Despite some occasional correspondence, Newton rarely traveled to London to meet with other Royal Society members. He continued his isolated research and became absorbed in studying both theology (the study of God and religion) and alchemy (the mystical philosophy that base elements can be changed into gold and that chemicals can be found that prolong life and heal disease). Then in 1684 some Royal Society members were debating planetary motion, the presumed attractive force of the sun that seemed to determine orbits, and the paths of comets, using Kepler's laws. They included Hooke, the architect Christopher Wren, and Edmund Halley (for whom Halley's comet would eventually be named). Halley wrote to Newton to ask about the mathematics involved in proving that some kind of attraction would determine the shape of the orbit and the speed of bodies pulled toward the sun. Hooke believed that an attraction—gravitation—applied to all objects in the solar system. Further, the power decreased with distance in an amount inversely proportional to the square of the distance between the sun and the object. But neither Hooke nor anyone else could prove this inverse-square law mathematically.

The Laws of Motion

Newton had worked out this relationship long ago, during the plague years he spent at Woolsthorpe, but his work was not organized or complete. He redid the mathematical proof and sent Halley a nine-page paper that connected the inverse-square law both to elliptical orbits and to all of Kepler's observations of planetary motion. Halley was thrilled and wanted to publish the paper, but Newton refused

The Fishes That Almost Thwarted the Laws of Motion

Without the enthusiasm of the young Edmund Halley—hired as a clerk for the Royal Society of London—Isaac Newton's *Principia* might never have been written or published. Newton was flattered by Halley's obvious admiration and respect, and it was Halley's pressure to publish his work for the world to see that persuaded Newton to complete the book. Then Halley had to pressure the Royal Society of London to get a promise to publish it. The society had recently ventured into publishing. It had paid for an expensive book to be printed called *The History of Fishes*. As it turned out, *The History of Fishes* was a flop and almost bankrupted the society. The organization was so leery of further financial loss with Newton's book that it reneged on its promise and informed Halley it would not pay for the publication of *Principia* after all. Instead, it gave Halley permission to have the book printed at his own expense. Halley was so certain of the book's importance that he agreed, even though he was not a wealthy man. Once in print, *Principia* was an overwhelming success, but that did not benefit Halley very much. Eventually, when the Royal Society could not even pay Halley a salary anymore, it began paying him in extra copies of *The History of Fishes*.

Force causes acceleration, which is a change in velocity, or speed in a specific direction. The greater the mass, the greater the amount of force required to accelerate that object. With a given amount of force, an object with a greater mass (a truck) will achieve less acceleration than an object of lesser mass (a ball).

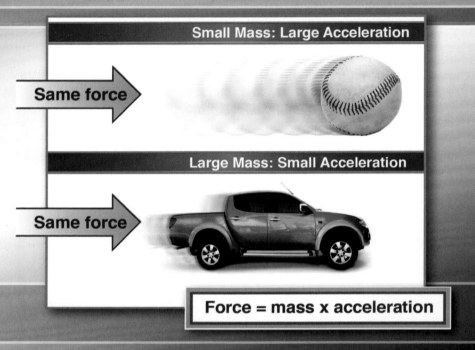

Small Mass: Large Acceleration

Same force

Large Mass: Small Acceleration

Same force

Force = mass x acceleration

Source: Bristol Public Schools, "Physics: Forces and Motion." www.bristol.k12.ct.us.

permission, saying he was not finished. He said, "Now I am upon this subject, I would gladly know the bottom of it before I publish my papers."[17] For the next several months, Newton devoted himself to more and more computations of heavenly motions, and his earlier ideas reached brilliant fruition. He conceived the theory of universal gravitation. He was sure it was right, but he needed more numerical facts to prove it. He wrote to Royal Society astronomer John Flamsteed asking to be sent observational data about two stars, the orbits of the moons of Jupiter, the paths of recently sighted comets, and even data on the tides of Earth's oceans. Then Newton wrote and calculated feverishly and copiously—thousands of words and reams of mathematical proofs. For the first time in his life, he was writing for others to read.

In 1686 Newton sent the first part of his finished work to Halley. It was an entire manuscript basing natural law on mathematical principles and explaining the forces of nature—Book 1 of his three-volume work titled *Philosophiae Naturalis Principia Mathematica* (*Mathematical Principles of Natural Philosophy*). Halley was amazed and overwhelmed. He wrote to Newton, "You will do yourself the honour of perfecting scientifically what all past ages have but blindly groped after."[18] Newton was already almost finished writing Book 2 and would soon follow up with Book 3. In July 1687, thanks to Halley, the complete book appeared in print, and it immediately revolutionized scientific and philosophical thought.

In Book 1 of *Principia* (as the book is usually called), Newton stated his now famous three laws of motion: The law of inertia, the law of acceleration, and the law of action and reaction. Modern

Who Is Sir Isaac Newton?

As an old man looking back on his life and discoveries, Isaac Newton often modestly denied his genius and spoke of himself with unassuming humility. He knew that there were many unanswered questions left about the universe and its workings. He once said, "I don't know what I may seem to the world, but, as to myself, I seem to have been only like a boy playing on the seashore, and diverting myself in now and then finding a smoother pebble or a prettier shell than ordinary, whilst the great ocean of truth lay all undiscovered before me." Despite his tremendous accomplishments, he still understood that much knowledge remained beyond his grasp.

Quoted in Edward Dolnick, *The Clockwork Universe: Isaac Newton, the Royal Society, and the Birth of the Modern World*. New York: HarperCollins, 2011. Kindle edition.

history professor Robert A. Hatch presents these laws in modern language:

1. Every body continues in its state of rest, or uniform motion in a straight line, unless it is compelled to change that state by forces impressed on it (inertia).

2. The change in motion is proportional to the motive [moving] force impressed and is made in the direction of the straight line in which that force is impressed (F = ma) [force equals mass times acceleration].

3. To every action [or force] there is always an opposed and equal reaction [or force].[19]

Following the presentation of these laws, Newton proceeded to prove mathematically that the axioms were true.

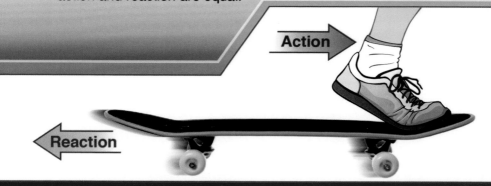

Newton's Third Law

The action of the foot pushes the rider forward off the skateboard, and the skateboard moves backward in an equal and opposite reaction. Distances traveled by both rider and skateboard are different because the masses are unequal, but the forces of action and reaction are equal.

Action

Reaction

In Book 3, subtitled *System of the World*, Newton used the laws of motion as the foundation for his law of universal gravitation. Hatch explains:

> Newton's law of universal gravitation states that $F = G\,Mm/R^2$; that is, that all matter is mutually attracted with a force (F) proportional to the product of their masses (Mm) and inversely proportional to the square of distance (R^2) between them. G [gravity] is a constant whose value depends on the units used for mass and distance. To demonstrate the power of his theory, Newton used gravitational attraction to explain the motion of the planets and their moons, the precession of equinoxes, the action of the tides, and the motion of comets. In sum, Newton's universe united heaven and earth with a single set of laws. It became the physical and intellectual foundation of the modern world view.[20]

From an Apple to Universal Laws

As an old man, Newton would tell the story of how he came to conceive of his laws of motion as he sat in the garden at Woolsthorpe and watched an apple fall from a tree. As he thought about the apple, he mused that there must be a "drawing power" in matter and that the Earth drew the apple downward, even as the apple drew the Earth in its direction. Then he wondered about this drawing power, "Why not as high as the Moon?"[21] These ideas, he said, led him to the mathematics that became the laws of motion and universal gravitation. No one today knows if the apple story is strictly true or if Newton was just making his discoveries more interesting with an enjoyable anecdote. It does not matter. The laws of motion apply equally and accurately to objects as different as apples and moons, and Isaac Newton proved it.

CHAPTER THREE

A Revolutionary Perspective

saac Newton's laws of motion gave rise to true science. This was not the science of the philosophers. Nor was it the science imposed by religious or ancient Greek authorities. It was the science of observation, experimentation, and mathematics. Very few people, however, could actually follow the mathematics underlying the laws of motion. The mathematical arguments and equations were so complex that Newton's book was almost unreadable, even for well-educated people. One Cambridge student, for instance, watched Newton walk by one day and said to a fellow student, "There goes the man that writt a book that neither he nor anybody else understands."[22] Of the few who could understand, some were critics, but most were in awe of the reasoning that fully explained the forces of nature. And the three laws of motion were simple, practical, and applicable to so many previously unsolvable scientific questions.

The Weird Concept of Gravity

The major issue for Newton's critics was the concept of *gravity*, upon which the laws of motion depended. Newton himself recognized that he did not know what gravity was or why it worked. He once wrote, "The Cause of Gravity is what I do not pretend to know."[23] Gravity was a mystery. It was, Newton claimed, a universal force of incredible power that traveled instantly across the vacuum of space and pulled planets into orbits, yanked comets toward the Earth, and jerked on Earth's oceans to cause the tides. Gravity meant that all matter attracted other matter, no matter how large or small. And all this occurred with no mechanism to transmit that force. It was something from nothing. To seventeenth-century mathematicians and scientists, gravity was no better as an explanation of natural events than magic or God's will.

One skeptic, the great German mathematician Gottfried Wilhelm von Leibniz, sneered about Newton, "He claims that a body attracts another, at whatever distance it may be, and that a grain of sand on earth exercises an attractive force as far as the sun, without any medium or means."[24] Newton did claim that, but as nonsensical as it seemed, the hypothesis of universal gravitation worked. Newton could not explain why, but reason and mathematics proved that it had to be true. Edward Dolnick explains, "Newton's mathematical laws gave correct answers—fantastically accurate answers—to questions that had long been out of reach, or they predicted findings that no one had ever anticipated. No one until Newton had explained the tides, or why there are two each day, or why the Earth bulges as it does, or why the moon jiggles as it orbits the Earth."[25] Newton's simple laws

Newton recognized that the gravitational forces exerted by the sun and the moon pulled on Earth's oceans. Because the moon is closer to Earth than the sun, it produces a greater pull. High and low tides occur when the moon is respectively closer to or farther from each ocean.

explained these and other natural phenomena—and the existence of gravity explained the why and how of these laws.

Conquering All Opposition

Newton did not handle opposition well. He was enraged by those who dared to criticize or question his theories and maintained life-long scientific feuds with them. He did all he could to crush his opposition and undermine their scientific credibility. Leibniz, who had also invented calculus independently of Newton, died almost forgotten, while Newton achieved renown throughout Europe. A similar fate befell Robert Hooke, who had suggested the idea of gravity but never was able to prove it. Newton gave him no credit for his ideas and maintained a bitter relationship with Hooke and with the Royal Society until Hooke died in 1703. That year Newton became presi-

A Soulless Theory

Poet and artist William Blake, who lived from 1757 to 1827, was an ardent critic of a Newtonian mechanical universe. It was not the scientific accuracy of the laws that he criticized; it was the philosophy that left no room for the imaginative, the emotional, and the meaningful beauty of God's creation. Blake condemned what he viewed as Isaac Newton's nonspiritual, rational view of a world reduced to natural laws. He thought Newton's science left no room for God. Blake once wrote, "He who sees the Infinite in all things sees God. He who sees the Ratio only, sees himself only." Blake produced a somewhat satirical portrait of Newton as a god-like figure bent over his compass and making diagrams while ignoring all the beauty of his environment and blind to the true meaning of anything. Blake was so horrified by the idea of reducing the universe to scientific facts and explanations that he insisted, "Art is the tree of life. Science is the tree of death."

William Blake, *There Is No Natural Religion*, Bartleby.com. www.bartleby.com.

Quoted in Mario Livio, "On William Blake's 'Newton,'" *The Blog, Huffington Post*, October 23, 2014. www.huffingtonpost.com.

dent of the Royal Society. By this time he wielded enough power and respect in the world of science to prevent anyone from even thinking about questioning his theories. Newton's final word on gravity, written in a later edition of *Principia* in 1713, was simple. He said, "And to us it is enough that gravity does really exist, and act according to the laws which we have explained, and abundantly serves to account for all the motions of the celestial bodies, and of our sea."[26] Especially for astronomers, the beauty of Newton's laws of motion lay in how practical they were. Newton's laws explained how to compute exactly the orbital periods of the planets, Jupiter's moons, and Earth's moon. He showed astronomers how to determine any satellite's greatest distance from its planet. Saying, "All the planets are heavy toward one another,"[27] he demonstrated mathematically that Jupiter's gravity influenced the orbit of Saturn, and the moon influenced the Earth. Everything attracts everything, according to its mass. That explained the wobble and slight changes in the orbits of planets—each orbit depended on the combined gravitational effects of every other body in the solar system, which could be described mathematically. It was possible to figure out what different objects would weigh on different planets. Astronomers could find the elliptical orbit of a planet just by knowing the focus point of the ellipse. They could predict where any celestial body would be at a certain point in time by observing the parabolic shape of its trajectory through the sky. At a time when comets were viewed as inexplicable omens or messages from God, Newton showed them to be natural phenomena. They were satellites of the sun with extremely large elliptical orbits, and they appeared in Earth's skies in predictable fashion. The universe was predictable; it operated like a perfect mechanical clock, and people could understand the rules by which it functioned.

The laws of motion were immediately applicable to earthly problems, too. For example, with a precise equation for determining the moon's position in the sky relative to the stars at any given moment,

> **WORDS IN CONTEXT**
>
> *parabolic*
>
> Having the form of a parabola—a curve, somewhat bowl-shaped and symmetrical, such as the path of a projectile.

Knowing how the moon travels in the nighttime sky and charting its position in relation to visible stars allowed sailors to compute their longitude at sea. Therefore Newton's laws of motion helped navigators more safely plot their courses across Earth's oceans.

sailors could calculate their longitude at sea. This meant that ships could determine their location and navigate the oceans more safely. For the military, application of the laws of motion meant knowing the correct angle to tilt a cannon so that a cannonball would travel the farthest. Using Newton's mathematics, Halley computed the angle at which to shoot a cannon so as to inflict maximum damage on a fortress high above it. The same mathematical formulas allowed Halley to accurately predict a solar eclipse in England in 1715. Events such as eclipses had long inspired fear. Halley's prediction demonstrated that an eclipse was neither mysterious nor supernatural. It was merely an example of Newton's natural laws.

A Genius Celebrity

Though largely incomprehensible to the general public, Newton's *Principia* found an enthusiastic audience among a select group of philosophers and mathematicians in Europe. They, in turn, interpreted the work—and its importance—for their less mathematically inclined peers. These people, too, became admirers of the brilliance behind *Principia*. In salons and coffeehouses throughout Europe, philosophers, natural philosophers (as scientists then called themselves), and educated thinkers gathered to discuss gravity, the laws of motion, and the orderly universe Newton had demonstrated. At the University of Oxford, astronomy professor David Gregory began teaching Newton's system of the universe; at Cambridge, students complained that Newton's departure prevented them from engaging in similar study and that they were instead being taught fiction.

Newton's reputation as a genius spread; he became a celebrity—idolized by the educated, the upper classes, and even royalty. The great French mathematician Marquis de l'Hôpital was shown a copy of *Principia* and is said to have cried, "Good god what a fund of knowledge there is in that book. . . . Does he eat & drink & sleep, is he like other men?"[28] Newton's fame was so great that he was elected as a member of the British Parliament for Cambridge University in 1689, and in 1705 he was knighted by Queen Anne. He also was appointed to be warden and master of the Royal Mint, became a wealthy man, and acquired a beautiful and comfortable London home, where he lived with a niece as his housekeeper.

When Newton died at age eighty-five in 1727 (1726 in the old English dating system), he was an honored, almost glorified figure. His body lay in state and was buried at Westminster Abbey. An inscribed monument was erected, and the Latin inscription reads (translated into English):

> Here is buried Isaac Newton, Knight, who by a strength of mind almost divine, and mathematical principles peculiarly his own, explored the course and figures of the planets, the paths of comets, the tides of the sea, the dissimilarities in rays of light, and, what no other scholar has previously

WORDS IN CONTEXT

trajectory

The curve of the path followed by a projectile or an object moving because of an external force.

imagined, the properties of the colours thus produced. Diligent, sagacious and faithful, in his expositions of nature, antiquity and the holy Scriptures, he vindicated by his philosophy the majesty of God mighty and good, and expressed the simplicity of the Gospel in his manners. Mortals rejoice that there has existed such and so great an ornament of the human race! He was born on 25th December 1642, and died on 20th March 1726.[29]

Spreading the Word

Newton's death did not put an end to the reverence and respect in which he and his revolutionary theories were held. His proofs that the natural world follows natural laws were disseminated throughout European society at most levels of education and culture, and they inspired a new way of thinking. In 1738, for example, the influential French philosopher and writer Voltaire wrote a book called *Elements of the Philosophy of Newton*. In this book, Voltaire attempted to explain universal gravitation and the laws of motion, along with Newton's discoveries about the nature of light and color, in a way that even ordinary, nonscientific people could understand. He was the first person to tell the fictitious story of the apple hitting Newton on the head—a tale he got from Newton's sister—and inspiring the concept of gravity.

From a scientific standpoint, Voltaire's book was not completely accurate. Voltaire did not really understand all the mathematics, but his popular book made Newton accessible to the masses and also, interestingly, made Newtonian theory acceptable to religious people. Many French religious figures thought that the mechanical universe described by Newton left no room for God. Some condemned Newton as an atheist. Newton, however, saw his natural laws as proof that God existed and had created the intricate universe in which His laws operated so perfectly. In his second edition of *Principia*, Newton wrote about God:

He endures always and is present everywhere, and by existing always and everywhere he constitutes duration [time] and space. Since each and every particle of space is *always*, and each and every indivisible moment of duration is *everywhere*, certainly the maker and lord of all things will not be *never* or *nowhere* . . . God is one and the same God always and every-where. He is omnipresent not only *virtually* but also *substan-tially*; for active power cannot subsist without substance.[30]

Voltaire wrote of Newton's devoutness and explained that New-ton's theories proved a divine design of the natural world. Voltaire ar-gued, for instance, that because comets could be hot and fiery even though they traveled too far away from the sun to be heated by it,

What Shape Is the Earth?

In 1736 the French Academy of Sciences sent two expeditions to measure the shape of the Earth and determine whether Isaac Newton's predictions of its shape were correct. Newton had calculated—based on his laws of gravitation and motion—that the Earth is not round but somewhat flat-tened at the poles and bulging at the equator. That is, the Earth is not a sphere but an oblate spheroid. The members of the Academy of Sciences wanted to prove that assertion. One expedition team, led by mathemati-cian Charles Marie de la Condamine, went to the Andes of South America. The other, headed by Pierre-Louis Moreau de Maupertuis, went to Lapland, the northernmost region of Finland. Both teams included mathematicians, astronomers, and skilled mapmakers and carried the most sophisticated measuring instruments available at the time. Maupertuis's team spent six-teen months in their icy environment making detailed measurements of degrees of latitude and longitude close to the pole. La Condamine and his scientific team spent six years climbing mountains, hauling equipment over cliffs, enduring huge storms, and coping with forest fires as they measured the Earth's curvature at the equator. When both teams finally returned with their data, they had the answer: Earth's equatorial diameter is 7,926 miles (12,756 km), but its polar diameter is 7,900 miles (12,714 km). This 26-mile (42-km) difference means the Earth is indeed an oblate spheroid, shaped something like a tomato. Newton was right.

comets proved God's hand in their design. The structure of comets, Voltaire said, "makes us equally admire the Wisdom of the Creator."[31] *Elements of the Philosophy of Newton* helped Christians accept Newton's science. The Catholic Jesuits, who controlled most French universities and schools of the period, dropped any resistance to Newtonian thinking and willingly taught the science as fact.

In the Western world after Newton's death, Newtonian thinking, and therefore science and scientists, gradually became the authority on how the world works and how the universe functions. In Italy, author Francesco Algarotti wrote a book called *Newtonianism for Ladies*, in which a collection of poems and conversations explain Newton's theories, referring to them as "The Light of Newtonianism"[32] and helping ordinary people see interest in science as fashionable. In England in 1761, writer John Newbery penned an extremely popular book for children under the pseudonym Tom Telescope. In the book, *The Newtonian System of Philosophy Adapted to the Capacities of Young Gentlemen and Ladies*, Tom is a young boy—highly moral and devoutly religious—who teaches the science of the solar system to his friends.

The Whipple Library of the University of Cambridge explains, "Tom Telescope, a child prodigy, was portrayed as a model of virtue, obtaining an understanding of God and His handiwork as he mastered the Newtonian system."[33]

How to Think like Newton

The natural laws that control the solar system or explain the ocean's tides, however, were not the only—or even the most important—part of Newtonian thinking. In *Principia*, Newton detailed and exemplified a whole new way of thinking. The laws of motion were not based on logic or deduction (like philosophy) but on experimentation, observation, and measurement, and any generalizations (or laws) were based on data empirically discovered. This was a scientific method, not a philosophical one. Any investigation to uncover a fact or rule of nature, Newton asserted, must be conducted under basic and fundamental "rules of philosophizing"—that is, rules for scientific reasoning. His first rule was, "No more causes of natural things should be admitted than are both true and sufficient to explain their phenomena." In other words, the scientific rule must be enough to explain an action accurately, and that is all that is needed. This meant, for instance, that the cause of the motion of the fall of an apple should be the same cause as the falling of a moon around Jupiter or a comet streaking through the solar system. A scientist should not search for many different explanations of motion if just one rule is enough to explain that motion. Newton elaborated further in his second rule: "The causes assigned to natural effects of the same kind must be, so far as possible, the same."[34] In other words, he explained, scientists should assume that a rock falling in Europe and one falling in America fall the same way for the same reason, and the reflection of light on Earth should be assumed to have the same cause as the reflection of light on the planets.

The third rule says that the characteristics of all bodies are the same when they are acted on by gravity. Bodies, no matter where they are in the universe, have hardness, size, thickness, and so on, but all respond to forces in the same way (by the laws of motion). Therefore,

One of Newton's philosophical "rules" maintained that natural, observable laws were applicable to all similar forms of motion. Therefore, the fall of a comet through space could be explained using the same gravitational principles that pertain to the fall of an apple from a tree.

according to Newton, when a scientist can formulate laws from experimentation for some objects or bodies, those laws apply as "the original and universal properties of all natural bodies." This is the idea of generalization—what is demonstrated for various objects through experimentation can be assumed to be true generally. Newton's fourth and last rule says that what has been experimentally proved should be assumed to be either "exactly or very nearly true"[35] until more data is discovered that would either refine the law to make it more accurate or demonstrate that there are exceptions to the rule.

A Newtonian Worldview

Newtonian thinking, then, is based on central scientific concepts, and for natural philosophers it had a profound impact. The universe is governed by unchanging laws that apply equally to all objects within it. Every aspect of any system is observable and with the right tools or mathematics can be discovered. The workings of the system can be reduced to basic rules, and these rules are simple and few. If the rules are correct and accurate, they can be used to calculate and predict what will happen. If physics could be reduced to natural laws, scientists and philosophers realized, so could every science. Phenomena such as electricity or magnetism could have their own natural laws. Perhaps even human beings were subject to natural laws that could be discovered and investigated.

The philosopher John Locke, a younger contemporary, friend, and admirer of Newton, believed that observation and scientific thinking could be used to understand the human mind. In *An Essay Concerning Human Understanding*, published in 1689, Locke applied Newtonian thinking to psychology, using the concepts of reductionism, simplicity, and generalization to develop rules about human nature. He theorized that just as gravity held the corpuscles (atoms) of all matter together, human minds were held together by the force of simple ideas—elementary, basic sensations—that led through association and learning to complex ideas. Mind and thought grow from experience, perceptions, and interaction with the environment. Locke's aim was to turn psychology into a Newtonian science. During the eighteenth century, people came to think that all observable phenomena were explainable and predictable; they became Newtonian thinkers.

44

CHAPTER FOUR

Simple Laws Equal Abundant Change

Newton's natural laws of motion and gravitation and Locke's adaptation of the concepts to people were the major influences that gave rise to the historical period in Western Europe known as the Enlightenment. Not only science, but also society and even politics changed permanently as people changed the ways they thought about themselves and the world.

Enlightened, Reasonable Religion

The Enlightenment was an eighteenth-century philosophical and cultural movement during which reason and empiricism gained ascendancy over religious dogma, faith, tradition, and mysticism. During the Enlightenment, most philosophers, scientists, and educated thinkers were not against religion, but they were opposed to taking religious dictates on faith. They were determined to base their religious views on reason. They believed that God was reasonable (as was proved by the laws of motion), and they refused to believe that God violated His own laws of nature. This meant that they rejected the magic, superstition, and mysticism that pervaded organized religion. Religious leaders of the time taught, for example, that floods, earthquakes, famines, and other natural disasters were God's punishments for human sins. Diseases were also sent by God, and cures and healings came through prayers, pleas for divine mercy, and God's forgiveness. Enlightened thinkers could not accept these traditional ideas. They were certain that the universe was orderly and that God did not randomly violate natural laws nor constantly intervene in His creation. Natural events had natural causes that could be investigated and explained with science. Science might not yet be able to determine the causes of disasters and diseases, but the causes were not supernatural. They were knowable, and reasonable people should not blame mysterious divine intervention for these events.

Many Enlightenment philosophers were deists. Deists believe in God as the creator of the intricate clockwork universe. God set the universe in motion—built the clock and wound it up—but did not then interfere with its workings. For the most part, deists do not believe in miracles or revelations from prophets or God's active participation in the lives of humanity. Their belief in God is based on reason. Their morality is logical and based on their own thinking. They believe their reasoning ability is a gift from God and that it can be used to understand Him and all things. Although Newton was not a deist, the deists of the Enlightenment based their religious views on Newton's arguments that all the natural order and beauty of the universe proved the existence of a supreme intelligent being who created the universe and everything in it. Natural law, as they saw it, demonstrated the existence of God.

Voltaire was a leading deist during the Enlightenment era. He vehemently criticized the irrationality, superstition, and dogma of organized religion and suggested that deism was "natural religion." He once argued, "What is faith? Is it to believe that which is evident? No. It is perfectly evident to my mind that there exists a necessary, eternal, supreme, and intelligent being. This is no matter of faith, but of reason." Voltaire considered himself a Newtonian and said of Newton's laws, "The more I glimpse of this philosophy, the more I admire it. One finds at each step that the whole universe is arranged by mathematical laws that are eternal and necessary."[36] He spoke for many in the Enlightenment era when he based his religious beliefs on Newton's science. As the era progressed, the superstition and magical thinking that had pervaded organized religion waned, while the spiritual and physical realms of thought gradually became separate.

Enlightened Politics and Government

Newtonian thinking permeated politics and culture in addition to religious philosophy. John Locke applied the concept of natural law to the psychology of human beings, concluding that each individual's desire to pursue happiness was a God-given law of nature and, therefore, a natural right. He argued logically that natural laws determine natural rights, and that every individual had the natural right to "life, health, liberty or possessions."[37] Furthermore, Locke declared, since humans are all born with the same capacity for learning and reasoning, humans are all equal. It is unreasonable to believe that monarchs have a divine right to rule or that God decreed the privileges of the aristocracy or that any government should be obeyed unquestioningly. Enlightenment thinkers applied these ideas to their demands for political reform and a restructuring of society along democratic lines.

Most historians consider Locke to be the philosophical father of the United States. Professor of astronomy and mathematics Kelly Cline says that Newton was the grandfather of the American Revolution. Locke's ideas about natural rights inspired Thomas Jefferson as he authored the Declaration of Independence and wrote of "life, liberty, and the pursuit of happiness." Many of America's founders (Benjamin Franklin, James Madison, and Alexander Hamilton, among others) studied Locke, but it was Newton's laws that formed the basis of Locke's natural rights. Cline says, "Personally, I think that the scientific revolution was an important factor in the birth of American freedom. . . . I think Newton would have been very happy to read our bill of rights and to see how freedom and scientific advancement have shaped the United States of America."[38]

Jefferson read and apparently understood Newton's *Principia* and believed that Newton was one of the greatest geniuses ever born. Modern history of science professor I. Bernard Cohen analyzes the Declaration of Independence and sees strong evidence of Newtonian thinking in Jefferson's words. Jefferson wrote in the preamble, for example, that people are entitled to equality and freedom by "the Laws of Nature and of Nature's God."[39] Cohen argues that "the evidence is overwhelming that the words 'laws of nature' would have been familiar

The concept of natural rights outlined in the Declaration of Independence has roots in the philosophy of John Locke. However, modern scholars believe Locke's ideas were influenced by Newton's natural laws and that some of the Founding Fathers were equally so influenced.

to Thomas Jefferson and to others of that day as a resonant echo of the science of Isaac Newton."[40] In a very real sense, Newton's laws of motion may have been responsible for the democratic republicanism of the United States and the constitutional freedoms now taken for granted in the Western world.

Astronomy and Halley's Comet

As the Western world became Newtonian in its thinking, reason and science became paramount. Newtonian thinking had a revolutionary effect on the sciences, especially on astronomy and the ability of astronomers to construct an accurate picture of the solar system. In 1705 Edmund Halley was applying Newton's new laws of motion and universal gravitation to the motions of bodies in the solar system. As he looked at the recorded data of the time, he noticed that the comets that were described in 1531, 1607, and 1682 all had extremely similar orbits. He concluded that all three sightings were of the same comet and calculated that the orbit of the comet brought it into Earth's view approximately once every seventy-six years. He accurately predicted the comet would return once again in 1758. Halley did not live to see his prediction come true—he died in 1742—but on Christmas night in 1758, the comet was spotted. Halley's prediction reinforced the validity of the laws of motion and earned the regular heavenly visitor its permanent name of Halley's comet.

> **WORDS IN CONTEXT**
>
> *republicanism*
>
> The ideology of governing a society or state as a republic, where the head of state is an elected representative of the people rather than the people being subjects of the head of state.

In the modern era the last visit of Halley's comet occurred in 1986. It was actually observed by astronomers in 1982. Using the powerful Hale Telescope at California's Palomar Observatory, they first spotted the comet when it was still beyond the orbit of Saturn and 1 billion miles (1.6 billion km) away from the sun—a feat not possible in Halley's time. As the comet approached Earth in 1986, two Russian spacecraft, one Japanese spacecraft, and one spacecraft from the European Space Agency flew out to meet it, making close flybys to photograph and analyze it. The fact that these spacecraft could intercept the comet accurately enough to study it is testimony to the value of the laws of motion and gravitation. Not only did astronomers know exactly where the comet would be at any given time, they also knew how to apply Newton's mathematics to the desired path of a spacecraft in order to intercept the comet. The trajectories of the spacecraft were calculated using Newton's formula for the law of gravitation: "Every particle of matter attracts every other particle of matter with a force directly proportional to the product of the masses and inversely proportional to the square of the distance between them."[41] John F. Santarius, a professor of engineering physics at the University of Wisconsin–Madison, explains, "Spacecraft today essentially all travel by being given an impulse [force] that places them on a trajectory in which they coast from one point to another, perhaps with other impulses or gravity assists along the way. The gravity fields of the Sun and planets govern such trajectories."[42] The next time the long, elliptical orbit of Halley's comet brings it past the Earth will be in 2061, and where it will be in the night skies on each date in June, July, and August of that year has already been plotted, thanks to Newton's laws of motion.

The orbit of Halley's comet brings it close enough to Earth to be observed every seventy-six years. The two-meter-long Giotto *probe (pictured), launched by the European Space Agency in 1982, was one of a few spacecraft that passed near enough to the comet in 1986 to take readings and photographs.*

The Planets and the Laws of Motion

The laws of motion gave astronomers the means to discover all the planets in the solar system at a time when only the five visible planets plus Earth were known. In 1781, when telescopes were considerably improved from Newton's time, the astronomer William Herschel was viewing the night sky in a search for binary, or double, stars. He saw a fuzzy object, which he first thought might be a comet. Then he realized that its movement through the sky was too slow for a comet. Over the next year, he watched the object move, plotted its positions, and determined that the object was in a planetary orbit eighteen times farther from the sun than Earth. It was the planet Uranus, with an orbital period of eighty-four Earth years—the first new planet to be discovered with a telescope and the first since ancient times. It was a further confirmation that Newton's laws were correct. People were stunned by the discovery of a new planet. King George III knighted Herschel for the discovery and appointed him court astronomer.

Uranus, however, presented a problem for astronomers. Over the next fifty years, they realized that it was not following the predicted orbit for its mass and distance from the sun. At first, astronomers applied the laws of motion to the problem by assuming that the slight pull of gravity from Jupiter and Saturn accounted for the variations in Uranus's orbit. Still, the mathematics did not work. A few astronomers began to wonder if the observed irregularities might be caused by an unknown planet orbiting further outside Uranus's orbit. In 1845 the French astronomer Urbain Jean Joseph Le Verrier decided to tackle the mystery. Le Verrier carefully studied the laws of motion and then used those laws to calculate exactly the mass, position, and path of the hypothetical planet that would account for the orbit of Uranus. On September 18, 1846, Le Verrier sent a letter to German astronomer Johann Galle at the Berlin Observatory detailing his mathematical results and asking Galle to look for the presumed planet in its predicted position in the night sky. Galle received the letter on September 23, and although he was skeptical, Le Verrier's work was so detailed and confident that Galle turned his telescope to the spot that very night. Within thirty minutes, within one degree of Le Verrier's predicted position, Galle barely made out a faint, fuzzy object. The next night he looked again and confirmed to his satisfaction that he had found the planet. Excitedly, Galle wrote back to Le Verrier, "The Planet whose position you indicated **really exists.** The same day I received your letter I found a star of the eighth magnitude that was not recorded on the excellent Carta Hora XXI [star map]. . . . The observation of the following day confirmed that it was the planet sought."[43] Thus, the planet Neptune was discovered by observing the effects of its gravity on other planets and with the mathematical calculations made possible by the laws of motion.

Still, as decades passed and larger and photography-capable telescopes were developed, scientists knew their picture of the solar system was not complete. Neptune, Uranus, and Saturn did not exactly follow the orbits predicted by the laws of motion. American astronomer Percival Lowell predicted a planet beyond Neptune that would account for the orbital variations of the outer planets. He searched for "Planet X," as he called it, but never found it. Lowell died in 1916, but other astronomers at the Lowell Observatory in Flagstaff, Arizona, were sure that Lowell's mathematics and predictions were correct. On March 13, 1930, the Lowell Observatory was able to announce its successful discovery of Planet X, which was subsequently named Pluto. The first astronomer to see it, Clyde W. Tombaugh, later wrote that "on the afternoon of February 18, 1930, I suddenly came upon the images of Pluto! The experience was an intense thrill, because the nature of the object was apparent at first sight."[44] Pluto was considered the ninth planet in the solar system from 1930 to 2006, when it was reclassified as a dwarf planet, part of the now recognized Kuiper Belt of icy bodies ringing the sun beyond the orbit of Neptune.

Satellites and Space Exploration

Today astronomers continue to learn about the nature of the objects in the solar system with spacecraft, orbiting satellites, and space probes. All space exploration is possible only because scientists have

Woodrow Wilson Objects to Newtonian Thinking

History of science professor I. Bernard Cohen says that Woodrow Wilson, the twenty-eighth president of the United States, was the first modern person to recognize that the US Constitution is a Newtonian document. Wilson published his thoughts on this subject in 1908 when he was president of Princeton University. He wrote, "The Constitution of the United States had been made under the dominion of the Newtonian Theory. You have only to read the papers of *The Federalist* to see that fact written on every page."

Wilson was a Progressive who argued that the Newtonian principles of the Constitution were outdated. He said that government and the Constitution should not be viewed as a rigid machine with insistence on things like the separation of powers to protect liberty. Instead, government and the laws should be viewed as a living organism that is open to reform. The United States should leave the Constitution and Newtonian thinking behind and move forward to a new type of evolving government that adjusts to the needs of the people. The federal government should have more power, Wilson believed, and the Constitution should be accepted as a living, growing document that adapts to changing times.

Quoted in Ronald J. Pestritto, *Woodrow Wilson and the Roots of Modern Liberalism.* Lanham, MD: Rowman & Littlefield, 2005, p. 119.

a mathematical understanding of the laws of motion. More than three hundred years ago, when Newton applied his laws of motion to cannonballs, he also imagined the workings of satellites in space, although he was thinking about Earth's moon and why it is a satellite. He envisioned cannonballs shot from more and more powerful cannons that traveled faster and faster. The faster the cannonballs traveled, the farther they would go before they fell to Earth. According to his first law of inertia, they would continue in their horizontal, straight line unless acted upon by an outside force—the gravity of Earth. The cannonballs would all fall to the Earth at the same rate, no matter what their speed (second law). But, Newton wondered, what would happen if one could get the cannon high above the Earth

The Apollo 11 *mission that brought American astronauts to the moon was made possible by Newtonian physics. The thrust of the rocket engines, the trajectory of the travel path, and the guidance of the landing craft rely on principles explained in Newton's laws of motion.*

and then fire the cannonball at a very high speed? Because the Earth is round, not flat, the Earth curves under the cannonball as it speeds along and then falls toward the ground. Edward Dolnick explains:

> If you launched it at just the right speed, then by the time the cannonball had fallen, say, four feet, the ground itself would

have fallen four feet below horizontal. And then what? The cannonball would continue on its journey forever, always falling but never coming any closer to the ground. Why? Because the cannonball always falls at the same rate, and the ground always curves beneath it at the same rate, so the cannonball falls and falls, and the Earth curves and curves, and the picture never changes. We have launched a satellite.

Newton pictured it all in 1687.[45]

Launching rockets carrying satellites into orbit or with other payloads is also dependent on the laws of motion. The rocket blasting off from the launchpad is moving from a state of rest (inertia) to a state of motion because of the force applied. The reason that the rocket takes off is that every action has an equal and opposite reaction (third law).

Beyond the Solar System

Isaac Newton's laws of motion and universal gravitation apply to much that astronomers observe in the universe. For instance, many stars revolve around a companion star. These binary star systems are common in Earth's Milky Way galaxy, and whether of similar or disparate sizes, their orbits around each other exactly match the laws of motion and gravity. Sometimes, astronomers observe a star moving in an elliptical orbit when no other star is seen. Nevertheless, they know according to Newton's laws that a companion star is there, too faint to be visible. Once that companion star's predicted position is calculated, astronomers are able to identify it using the radiation it is emitting beyond visible light.

All the stars in the Milky Way galaxy are rotating around a common point, or focus, under the influence of gravity. In the center of the galaxy, the stars rotate in particularly tight, high-speed orbital paths. This observation suggests that there is a powerful gravitational pull at the galactic center. Twenty-first-century astronomers now understand that the pull is due to a massive black hole. Scientists have named this black hole Sagittarius A* (pronounced "Sagittarius A star"). The stars orbiting Sagittarius A* follow paths predicted by the laws of motion.

As the rocket expels gas from the engine (action), the rocket pushes on the gas, and the gas pushes on the rocket, so the rocket's reaction is movement in the opposite direction—upward.

Applying the principles of the laws of motion in a mathematically detailed way also means that scientists can plot paths and trajectories for space missions. Every inch of the way of NASA's 1969 *Apollo 11* trip to the moon, the calculations for a successful journey were based on the laws of motion and universal gravitation. Sending exploratory missions and probes to Mars and for flybys of Jupiter is made possible by Newtonian physics. Newton's simple natural laws not only explain the universe, they allow scientists to explore and function with precision within it.

CHAPTER FIVE

The Laws of Motion and the Contemporary World

By the twentieth century Isaac Newton's universal gravitation and laws of motion were accepted unquestioningly throughout the world. Then in 1905 physicist Albert Einstein analyzed the assumptions underlying the three laws of motion and mathematically determined that they were only approximations of reality. In 1915 he did the same with universal gravitation, demonstrating that it was only approximately correct. The laws of motion do not hold when velocity approaches the speed of light. And gravity is not a constant over unchanging space and time, as Newton had supposed. It is not an absolute, straight force but a curvature in space-time. Matter is not even an unchanging constant in the universe. It is equivalent to energy, and at the subatomic level it can be converted to energy, such as at the heart of the sun or in a nuclear bomb.

Was Newton Wrong?

Einstein's relativity theory gave new meaning to space-time and gravity. At this point, many people wondered if Newton had been overturned and Newtonian thinking was dead. In 1930 the playwright and intellectual George Bernard Shaw said of the theory of relativity:

> Newton invented a straight line, and that was the law of gravitation, and when he had invented this, he had created a universe which was wonderful in itself. . . . For 300 years we believed in that Newtonian universe as I suppose no system has been believed in before. . . . [But] the world is not

a rectilinear world: It is a curvilinear world. The heavenly bodies go in curves because that is the natural way for them to go, and so the whole Newtonian universe crumpled up and was succeeded by the Einstein universe.[46]

In reality, however, Einstein did not overturn Newton's laws of motion. He adjusted and added to Newton's universe with more precise knowledge. When not dealing with things that are very small (like subatomic particles) or very fast (approaching the speed of light) or with very strong gravity fields (such as no one on Earth could ever experience), Newtonian physics—far from crumpling up—are still applicable and true. Einstein himself explained, "Let no one suppose that the mighty work of Newton can really be superseded by this or any other theory. His great and lucid ideas will retain their unique significance for all time as the foundation of our whole modern conceptual structure in the sphere of natural philosophy."[47]

The laws of motion and universal gravitation remain the backbone of much of the physics done today. The science of mechanics—the applied mathematics dealing with motion and the forces producing motion—is based on the laws of motion. Einstein may have shown that the three laws of motion are only approximations of reality, but Newton's laws work so well to describe almost everything in day-to-day life that they remain the predominant explanation for all sorts of motion. For example, Newtonian physics describes a car's acceleration, the path of a baseball thrown into the air, and the orbit of a satellite around the Earth. Today scientists refer to Newtonian physics as "classical mechanics," and the three laws of motion are the foundation of classical mechanics. They describe, explain, and predict the world, and without classical mechanics modern society would not exist. From cars to airplane travel to sports to satellites that transmit television signals, life today illustrates and depends on the reality of the laws of motion.

Although Albert Einstein found that there are limits to Newtonian physics, the mechanics of Newton's laws still hold true in most instances, such as in the arc of a pitched baseball. Newtonian physics breaks down only when science deals with extremes of speed, size, and gravitational field.

Accomplished with Newton's Laws

The story of a passenger jet in trouble spectacularly demonstrates the laws of motion in action. On the afternoon of January 15, 2009, US Airways Flight 1549 took off from New York City's LaGuardia Airport with 155 people aboard. Its pilot was Captain Chesley Sullenberger. Shortly after takeoff, the plane hit a large flock of Canada geese. Both engines were destroyed, resulting in a complete loss of thrust. Sullenberger later remembered, "I could feel the momentum stopping, and the airplane slowing."[48] Repeated efforts by copilot Jeffrey Skiles to reignite the engines failed.

From an altitude of about 3,000 feet (914 m), the plane was descending at a rate of 1,000 feet (305 m) per minute. It was a horrifying situation. The experienced captain says, "The first thing I did was lower the plane's nose to achieve the best glide speed. For all of us on board to survive, the plane had to become an efficient glider."[49] Then he made the grim but confident decision to attempt a water landing in the Hudson River. It was the only smooth, long, wide-enough space within gliding reach where the plane might return to Earth without crashing. With the plane 900 feet (274 m) above the George Washington Bridge (which spans the river) and about ninety seconds before touchdown, Sullenberger announced to the passengers over the public address system, "This is the captain. Brace for impact!"[50]

WORDS IN CONTEXT

thrust

A reaction force that causes an object to move forward in a certain direction.

Sullenberger glided the plane toward the water while Skiles lowered the flaps to slow it in preparation for landing. The captain explains, "As we came in for a landing, without thrust, the only control I had over our vertical path was pitch—raising or lowering the nose of the plane. My goal was to maintain a pitch attitude that would give the proper glide speed. In essence, I was using the earth's gravity to provide the forward motion of the aircraft, slicing the wings through the air to create lift."[51] Sullenberger succeeded, although he could not slow the plane enough for the best landing. With its nose up, the plane touched the river, with the rear hitting the water first. That impact was violent enough to severely tear the metal of the plane's rear fuselage, but the wings stayed even and straight, and the plane slid along the water to a complete stop. All the passengers and crew escaped into rescue boats, with only a few minor injuries.

The Miracle on the Hudson

The water ditching of Flight 1549 without loss of life came to be known as the "miracle on the Hudson." But while the perfect landing

Glide Ratio

The glide ratio is the distance that an aircraft can travel in relation to the altitude it is losing when the plane has lost all thrust. It is computed with a complicated formula that considers lift, velocity, time, and the height of the plane above the ground. The glide ratio of Flight 1549 explains why Captain Chesley Sullenberger did not attempt to turn his plane around and return to the airport when he lost thrust. He had to consider his altitude (quite low for the mass of the plane), the rate of the change in velocity (acceleration was dropping), and his distance from the airport (while gliding over a densely populated area with tall buildings). Sullenberger remembers:

> Looking out the window, I saw how rapidly we were descending. My decision would need to come in an instant: Did we have enough altitude and speed to make the turn back toward the airport and then reach it before hitting the ground? There wasn't time to do the math, so it's not as if I was making altitude-descent calculations in my head. But I was judging what I saw out the window and creating, very quickly, a three-dimensional mental model of where we were.

Sullenberger's expertise included extensive mathematical experience with aviation calculations based on the laws of motion. His judgment was based in part on connecting the mathematics to real-world situations. Much later, in flight simulators, trained pilots re-created Flight 1549's situation and tried to make it back to the airport. All of them failed.

Captain Chesley "Sully" Sullenberger with Jeffrey Zaslow, *Highest Duty: My Search for What Really Matters.* New York: HarperCollins, 2009, pp. 223–24.

in a terrible crisis required deft handling by the pilots, it was actually a classic demonstration of the laws of motion at work. Relying on their skill and expertise, Sullenberger and Skiles overcame the dire emergency by making use of the laws of motion and universal gravitation. An aircraft flies because its wings push air down, and with an equal and opposite reaction, the air pushes back, creating lift. At the same time, it moves forward because the engines push air back with enough force to counter the drag of the moving air. This is thrust.

Newton's first law of motion explains why a plane stays at a constant velocity (speed in a specific direction). Inertia means that an apple stays motionless on a table unless acted on by an outside force. But it also means that an aircraft in motion stays in motion unless the forces acting on it become unequal. A plane in flight has the right lift and thrust to keep it in balance with the forces of gravity and drag. Those forces cancel each other out, and the plane maintains a constant speed and altitude because of inertia.

When Flight 1549 lost its engines and all thrust, the forces became unbalanced. As thrust was lost, speed decreased, as would be predicted by Newton's second law. Without the force, acceleration (velocity divided by a change in time) was lost. However, the wings continued to supply lift, according to Newton's third law. The plane did not drop like a stone toward the Earth. It glided downward because of gravity, while using the push of air on the wings to maintain lift. Wings can stall, however, if the push of air downward is not in balance with the speed of the plane. Lowering the nose downward,

Rescue craft surround US Airways Flight 1549 as it remains afloat after crash landing into the Hudson River on January 15, 2009. The pilots used basic Newtonian mechanics to angle the plane so that maximum lift was maintained, allowing the craft to glide, rather than plummet, into the water.

as Sullenberger did at the first loss of thrust, puts the wings back into the right position to push air downward and to glide with maximum air pushing upward on the plane.

Raising and lowering the nose of the plane is called pitch. As the force of gravity brought the plane down to a landing, Sullenberger adjusted the pitch to keep the wings maintaining lift, while at the same time raising the nose to increase the drag of air on the plane and slow it down for contact with the water. The flaps that Skiles lowered also increased drag while increasing lift. When the belly of the plane came into contact with the water, the plane's motion was essentially abruptly interrupted by an outside force—the river surface. The impact to the plane's belly was enough to tear it apart because of the plane's momentum. Momentum is the amount of motion, and it is mathematically measured by mass times velocity. Momentum and gravity interact, according to the universal law of gravitation, to increase the force of impact. The rear of the plane experienced most of the force of hitting the river, and it was the momentum—not actually gravity—that caused the damage to the plane.

> **WORDS IN CONTEXT**
>
> *glide*
> To fly without engine power and descend gradually in a controlled flight.

Flight 1549 experienced a hard landing but not a violent one. Most of the plane was undamaged. Sullenberger maintained the gliding from the wings all the way through the landing, so the plane slid along the water's surface rather than slamming or diving into it. Finally, the plane came to a stop because of the forces of gravity and friction of the water. The people in the plane were, of course, moving as fast as the airplane. At the fraction of the second after the plane experienced a significant slowing of forward motion upon touching the surface of the water, the people continued to fly forward because of inertia. This was why Sullenberger had told them to brace for impact. And it was why people were wearing seatbelts. The seatbelts held people in their seats as their bodies continued to move forward according to the first law. The muscle resistance of their bodies applied the force that helped them resist forward motion and avoid hitting the seat backs in front of them. Newton's laws of motion determined the success of the landing on the Hudson.

Safety Designs from the Laws of Motion

The same laws of motion account for the seatbelts and airbags in cars today. When a car traveling 50 miles an hour (80 kph) slams into a telephone pole or a brick wall, the car stops moving, but the people inside—who are also traveling at 50 miles an hour—keep moving because of inertia. Seatbelts provide the force that stops the inertial forward motion instead of the external force of the windshield or the dashboard. Seatbelts, however, only restrain the torso. Even when the body stops, the head continues moving forward. That is why airbags were developed. Airbags work by increasing the time until impact and decreasing the force of the impact. Airbags are made to deflate as soon as an object (like a head) hits them. This is because of the third law of motion: A solid airbag hit by a head would hit the head back with the same amount of force. It would be as bad as hitting the dashboard. As it is, the escaping air from the airbag means that the impact is minimized and a person's head has time to decelerate safely. Injury risk is greatly reduced. The National Highway Traffic Safety Administration estimates that 39,976 lives were saved by airbags in the United States between 1987 and 2012.

Natural Laws and Sports

Application of the laws of motion also has relevance to the risk of injury in activities such as sports. In Thoroughbred horse racing, for example, a horse at rest at the starting gate uses the force of its muscles to push off with its hooves from the gate and accelerate quickly. Newton's second law—F = ma—explains the action. The horse's body is the mass (which remains constant during the race). The force is supplied by the horse's muscles and results in a change in velocity, which creates acceleration. The greater the force, the greater the acceleration. The jockey on the horse's back is subject to the laws of motion, as well. The jockey's seat is in contact with the horse, so as the horse accelerates, the jockey's lower torso moves forward. At the same time, the jockey's upper body tends to remain at rest because of Newton's first law. An unprepared jockey would thus seem to lean backward, slow the horse-jockey unit down, and lose the race. If the jockey jerked too far backward, he or she might even fall and be in-

Like a Rocket

Isaac Newton's third law operates in the same way for a skateboard as for a spaceship launch. Both are at rest until a force overcomes inertia, and both have an equal and opposite reaction. A rocket's gases push on the rocket when the gases are ejected from the engine. A boy, as an example, can stand on a skateboard and then push off of it. The force in this case is the muscular motion of the boy's foot as he hops forward to the ground. The skateboard moves backward in the opposite direction of the boy's push off. Probably, the skateboard moves farther in distance than the boy, but this is not because the reaction was greater than the action. It is because the boy's mass is so much greater than the mass of the board. Action and reaction were equal.

jured. A professional jockey is well aware of this problem, however, and that is why he or she uses the force of muscles to lean forward as the horse breaks for its start.

Inertia can be disastrous in show-jumping sports when something goes wrong. In order to take off for a jump, the horse pushes against the ground with its back legs (and the ground pushes back) to launch its mass upward and forward. This is acceleration. Once its hooves leave the ground, the horse is no longer using any muscular force, and it becomes a projectile. The only force acting on a projectile is gravity. The trajectory of any projectile is a parabola—like Newton's cannonball. The path of the horse's body in the air is an arc, as its momentum carries it vertically and forward while gravity pulls it down. This means that, as the horse lands on the other side of the obstacle, it lands at an angle aiming downward, at the end of its parabolic flight. If a rider does not use muscular force to stop forward motion when the horse's forward motion stops, he or she will continue moving forward and likely end up on the ground with a serious head or neck injury. Car and airplane crashes, riding accidents, and even collisions between football players all can be understood and mitigated with an appreciation of how momentum, velocity, and damaging impacts are all functions of the laws of motion. Helmets, airbags, seatbelts, and aerodynamically crafted wings are just some of the protections developed by engineers to help people deal with the real-life perils of natural laws.

Engineering Designs

The laws of motion and universal gravitation are still the basis of modern engineering. An understanding of the laws of motion determines the design of any vehicle, from a sports car to a train to a rocket. The design of a fuel-efficient automobile, for example, is based in large part on reducing its mass and thus reducing the force required to achieve acceleration and velocity (the second law of motion). Buildings and highway bridges are superstructures engineered to be earthquake resistant on the basis of the second law of motion. Engineers calculate the mass of the structure, the force of the earthquake it must withstand, the possible acceleration of the structure under the effect of the force, and the possible acceleration of the ground due to the earthquake. Then they are able to design the superstructure to prevent its damage and failure during a catastrophic event.

Dean Kamen says that the laws of motion are also the keys to the design and operation of his Segway Personal Transporter. He explains, "It's the rules of the world. It's what nature put here, how do we as humans understand that? Technology is taking that understanding, those tools, and building with those tools and in that framework of understanding, the products that we all want to use to make our lives better."[52]

Amusement park rides are further examples of the laws of motion at work. Roller coasters, for instance, are based on the fact that objects in motion tend to stay in motion (first law). The coaster builds up momentum as it gets to the top of the first hill, often pulled by a chain under the track or with a motor that pulls the coaster up the hill with magnets. Then gravity takes over as the coaster accelerates down the guiding track. Usually, each subsequent hill is smaller than the

Modern engineers apply Newton's second law of motion to the construction of marvels like the Golden Gate Bridge in San Francisco. They recognize that these structures must be built to withstand earthquakes and other disasters, so they devise ways to distribute or redirect the forces involved.

first hill. Through inertia, the coaster cars accelerate up the next hills while slowing due to the force of gravity and then accelerate down the hills while increasing in velocity. The fluctuation in acceleration is what makes the roller coaster so enjoyable.

Indebted to Newton

The modern mathematician and cosmologist Hermann Bondi once said of Newton and his laws, "The tools that he gave us stand at the root of so much that goes on now."[53] Modern life is Newtonian, and even without realizing it, people incorporate the ideas and language into their views of the world. People speak of "the gravity of a situation," "the force of an argument," "the inertia of government bureaucracy," or "a football team's momentum" and are barely aware that they are thinking in terms of natural laws. Without the laws of motion, not only technology but even modern thought would not exist.

SOURCE NOTES

Introduction: The Origin of the Modern Age

1. *Science of Everyday Things*, "Laws of Motion," Encyclopedia.com, 2002. www.encyclopedia.com.
2. Quoted in Eric W. Weisstein, "Newton, Isaac (1642–1727)," ScienceWorld, 2007. http://scienceworld.wolfram.com.

Chapter One: "On the Shoulders of Giants"

3. Quoted in International Space Hall of Fame, "Nicolaus Copernicus," New Mexico Museum of Space History. www.nmspace museum.org.
4. Quoted in International Space Hall of Fame, "Nicolaus Copernicus."
5. Quoted in Edward Dolnick, *The Clockwork Universe: Isaac Newton, the Royal Society, and the Birth of the Modern World*. New York: HarperCollins, 2011. Kindle edition.
6. Quoted in Nick Greene, "Biography of Giordano Bruno," About .com. http://space.about.com.
7. Quoted in Dolnick, *The Clockwork Universe*.
8. Dolnick, *The Clockwork Universe*.
9. Galileo Galilei, *The Sidereal Messenger of Galileo Galilei and a Part of the Preface to Kepler's Dioptrics: Containing the Original Account of Galileo's Astronomical Discoveries*, trans. Edward Stafford Carlos. London: Rivingtons, Oxford and Cambridge, 1880, p. 11.
10. Quoted in David Eckstein, "Galileo Galilei's Principle of Relativity," Relativity, 2009. www.relativity.li.
11. Dolnick, *The Clockwork Universe*.

Chapter Two: Isaac Newton

12. Quoted in Richard Westfall, *The Life of Isaac Newton*. New York: Cambridge University Press, 1993, p. 10.
13. Quoted in James Gleick, *Isaac Newton*. New York: Vintage, 2004. Kindle edition.

14. Gleick, *Isaac Newton*.
15. Quoted in Gleick, *Isaac Newton*.
16. Quoted in Gleick, *Isaac Newton*.
17. Quoted in Gleick, *Isaac Newton*.
18. Quoted in W.W. Rouse Ball, *An Essay on Newton's "Principia."* London: Macmillan, 1893, p. 171.
19. Robert A. Hatch, "Sir Isaac Newton," University of Florida, 1998. http://users.clas.ufl.edu.
20. Hatch, "Sir Isaac Newton."
21. Quoted in Steve Connor, "The Core of Truth Behind Sir Isaac Newton's Apple," *Independent* (London), January 18, 2010. www.independent.co.uk.

Chapter Three: A Revolutionary Perspective

22. Quoted in Gleick, *Isaac Newton*.
23. Quoted in Steve Nakoneshny, "The Complexity of Newton," Galilean, 2007. www.galilean-library.org.
24. Quoted in Dolnick, *The Clockwork Universe*.
25. Dolnick, *The Clockwork Universe*.
26. Quoted in Dolnick, *The Clockwork Universe*.
27. Quoted in Gleick, *Isaac Newton*.
28. Quoted in Brian L. Silver, *The Ascent of Science*. New York: Oxford University Press, 1998, p. 37.
29. Quoted in Westminster Abbey, "Sir Isaac Newton," 2015. www.westminster-abbey.org.
30. Quoted in Andrew Janiak, "Newton's Philosophy," *Stanford Encyclopedia of Philosophy*, May 6, 2014. http://plato.stanford.edu.
31. Quoted in Bernard Lightman, "Unbelief," in *Science and Religion Around the World*, ed. John Hedley Brooke and Ronald L. Numbers. New York: Oxford University Press, 2011, p. 257.
32. Quoted in Whipple Library, "Newton for Ladies," University of Cambridge, 2011. www.hps.cam.ac.uk.
33. Whipple Library, "Newton for Children: Tom Telescope," University of Cambridge, 2011. www.hps.cam.ac.uk.
34. Quoted in Gleick, *Isaac Newton*.

35. Quoted in John Mason Good, Olinthus Gilbert Gregory, and Newton Bosworth, *Pantologia: A New (Cabinet) Cyclopaedia*, vol. 4. London, 1819.

Chapter Four: Simple Laws
Equal Abundant Change

36. Quoted in Sveinbjorn Thordarson, "Voltaire, d'Holbach and the Design Argument," University of Edinburgh, August 2008. www .sveinbjorn.org.

37. Quoted in Kelly Cline, "How Isaac Newton's Science Inspired the American Revolution," *Helena (MT) Independent Record*, May 4, 2011. http://helenair.com.

38. Cline, "How Isaac Newton's Science Inspired the American Revolution."

39. Quoted in I. Bernard Cohen, *Science and the Founding Fathers: Science in the Political Thought of Thomas Jefferson, Benjamin Franklin, John Adams, and James Madison*. New York: Norton, 1997, p. 110.

40. Cohen, *Science and the Founding Fathers*, p. 113.

41. Quoted in John F. Santarius, "Lecture #9: You Can Get There from Here! Spacecraft Trajectories," Fusion Technology Institute, University of Wisconsin–Madison, February 8, 1999. http://fti.neep.wisc.edu.

42. Santarius, "Lecture #9."

43. Quoted in J.J. O'Connor and E.F. Robertson, "Urbain Jean Joseph Le Verrier," School of Mathematics and Statistics, University of St. Andrews, Scotland, January 2014. www-history.mcs .st-and.ac.uk.

44. Quoted in J.J. O'Connor and E.F. Robertson, "Mathematical Discovery of Planets," School of Mathematics and Statistics, University of St. Andrews, Scotland, September 1996. www-history.mcs.st-and.ac.uk.

45. Dolnick, *The Clockwork Universe*.

Chapter Five: The Laws of Motion
and the Contemporary World

46. Quoted in Michael Holroyd, "Albert Einstein, Universe Maker," *New York Times*, March 14, 1991. www.nytimes.com.

47. Quoted in Gleick, *Isaac Newton*.
48. Captain Chesley "Sully" Sullenberger with Jeffrey Zaslow, *Highest Duty: My Search for What Really Matters*. New York: Harper-Collins, 2009, p. 209.
49. Sullenberger with Zaslow, *Highest Duty*, p. 214.
50. Sullenberger with Zaslow, *Highest Duty*, p. 235.
51. Sullenberger with Zaslow, *Highest Duty*, p. 237.
52. Quoted in *Quest*, "Inventors of New England," transcript, Maine Public Broadcasting Network. www.mpbn.net.
53. Quoted in Gleick, *Isaac Newton*.

IMPORTANT PEOPLE IN THE HISTORY OF THE LAWS OF MOTION

Nicolaus Copernicus: The sixteenth-century mathematician and astronomer who theorized a model of the universe that placed the sun, instead of the Earth, at the center of the universe. Copernicus's work laid the foundation for future scientists to build an understanding of the motions of bodies in the solar system.

René Descartes: Descartes developed analytic geometry and the Cartesian coordinate system still in use today. Without his mathematics, Isaac Newton could not have developed the calculus that allowed a calculation of motion and changes in positions over time.

Galileo Galilei: Galileo is generally recognized as the forefather of the sciences of motion and astronomy. He was a mathematician, engineer, astronomer, and philosopher who quantified the behavior of falling objects and formulated a universal law of acceleration. He developed a telescope capable of viewing the five known planets, the moons of Jupiter, and the geography of Earth's moon and used those observations and mathematics to prove the truth of the Copernican system.

Edmund Halley: A member of the Royal Society of London, Halley was an astronomer and mathematician who was trying to quantify planetary motion when he discovered that Isaac Newton had already addressed the problem successfully. In awe of Newton's mathematics, Halley was instrumental in persuading Newton to share and publicize his findings and was almost single-handedly responsible for the publication of Newton's *Principia*. Later Halley would apply Newton's laws of motion to the study of comets. In 1716 he also used Newton's laws to accurately determine the distance from the Earth to the sun.

Johannes Kepler: In the early 1600s Kepler proposed three laws of planetary motion, stating that planets orbit the sun in an ellipse, that the speed of a planet's orbit changes as it gets closer to and farther from the sun in that ellipse, and that a planet's orbital period depends on its distance from the sun. Kepler could not explain these laws, although he did develop the mathematical equations to describe them.

Gottfried Wilhelm von Leibniz: A contemporary of Isaac Newton, Leibniz was a mathematician who independently invented calculus and became Newton's biggest critic, both over the invention of calculus and the concept of *gravity*. The antagonism between the two men escalated into a lifelong dispute, which Newton won. Nevertheless, the notation system used in calculus today is Leibniz's elegant one, not Newton's cumbersome one.

John Locke: The English philosopher who is credited with having a seminal influence on the Enlightenment era. A younger contemporary of Isaac Newton, Locke applied Newtonian theory to human beings, politics, and psychology and postulated the natural laws that govern people and society, including natural individual rights, freedom, and equality. Locke is often considered the philosophical father of the United States.

Isaac Newton: One of the most brilliant and influential scientists of all time, Newton developed and mathematically proved the three laws of motion and universal gravitation. His groundbreaking book, *Philosophiae Naturalis Principia Mathematica* (*Mathematical Principles of Natural Philosophy*), is usually considered the greatest scientific book ever written. In it Newton explains the motions of the planets and their orbits, the force of gravity, the orbits of comets, the motion of the tides, the shape of the Earth, and the motion of the moon. In addition, he invented calculus and made many other contributions to mathematics, proposed new theories of light and color, invented the reflecting telescope, and basically invented the modern scientific method.

FOR FURTHER RESEARCH

Books

Margaret J. Anderson, *Isaac Newton: Greatest Genius of Science*. New York: Enslow, 2015.

Fred Bortz, *Johannes Kepler and the Three Laws of Planetary Motion*. New York: Rosen, 2014.

Fred Bortz, *Laws of Motion and Isaac Newton*. New York: Rosen, 2014.

Schrylet Cameron and Carolyn Craig, *Scientific Theories, Laws, and Principles*. Quincy, IL: Mark Twain Media, 2011.

Jane P. Gardner, *Physics: Investigate the Mechanics of Nature*. White River Junction, VT: Nomad, 2014.

Paul W. Hightower, *Galileo: Genius Astronomer*. New York: Enslow, 2015.

Kristen Petersen, *Understanding the Laws of Motion*. New York: Cavendish Square, 2015.

Websites

Beginner's Guide to Aeronautics, NASA Glenn Research Center (www.grc.nasa.gov/WWW/k-12/airplane). Learn how aircraft fly, how the laws of motion relate to flight, from a rocket to a plane to a kite to a baseball, and what aerodynamics is all about. The site offers information for younger kids as well as for older students.

Engineer Girl (www.engineergirl.org). Developed by the National Academy of Engineering and sponsored by Lockheed Martin, this site encourages people to consider a career in engineering. It offers information about what engineers do, what it is like to be an engineer, and the many fun projects possible with engineering today.

Liftoff to Learning: Newton in Space (https://archive.org/details/lift off_to_learning_3_newton_in_space). This short NASA video shows how the laws of motion apply to spaceflight. Astronauts perform simple demonstrations of the laws of motion in the environment of space.

Newton Project (www.newtonproject.sussex.ac.uk). Dedicated to all things Newton, this site offers photocopies of Isaac Newton's handwritten letters and texts, extensive biographical information, and a "tour" with descriptions and artwork from Newton's time, along with accounts from his contemporary biographers.

Physics4Kids! (www.physics4kids.com). This site discusses physics concepts in a way that is easy to understand. It covers not only motion but also topics such as heat, electromagnetism, and light.

Science360 Video (http://science360.gov). Watch videos about the latest discoveries in science, technology, engineering, and math at this website sponsored by the National Science Foundation. In the "Science of NFL Football" section, for example, visitors can watch videos explaining how the laws of motion relate to success in the sport. And in the "Little Shop of Physics" section, videos explain motion through interesting experiments anyone can do.

INDEX

PICTURE CREDITS

ABOUT THE AUTHOR

Toney Allman holds degrees from Ohio State University and the University of Hawaii. She currently lives in Virginia, where she enjoys a rural lifestyle as well as researching and writing about a variety of topics for students.